W9-DFZ-036

The Evolution of Government and Politics in

EGYPT

EGYPT

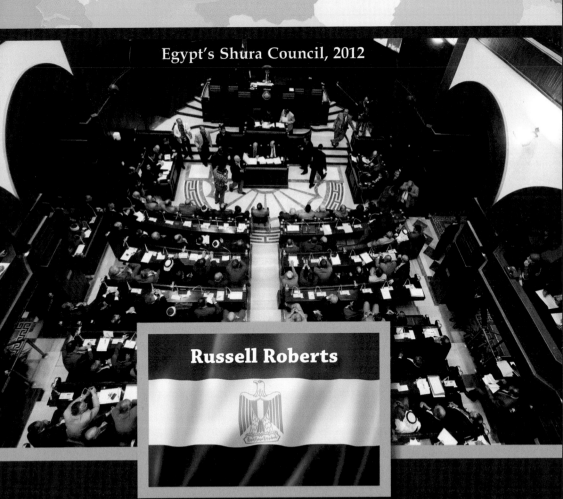

Egypt's Shura Council, 2012

Russell Roberts

Mitchell Lane
PUBLISHERS
P.O. Box 196
Hockessin, DE 19707

The Evolution of Government and Politics in

CHINA
EGYPT
FRANCE
GERMANY
GREECE
IRAQ
ITALY
NORTH AND SOUTH KOREA
THE UNITED KINGDOM
VENEZUELA

Printing 1 2 3 4 5 6 7 8 9

Library of Congress
Cataloging-in-Publication Data

Roberts, Russell, 1953–
 The evolution of government and politics in
Egypt / by Russell Roberts.
     pages cm. — (The evolution of
government and politics)
 Includes bibliographical references and index.
 ISBN 978-1-61228-585-6 (library bound)
1. Egypt—Politics and government. I. Title.
 JQ3831.R635 2015
 320.962—dc23

                                    2014008867

eBook ISBN: 9781612286228

                                    PBP

Contents

Chapter 1
Coup! 4

Chapter 2
The Land of the Pharaohs..10

Chapter 3
Struggle for Independence..18

Chapter 4
From Tyranny to Democracy to . . . ? 26

Chapter 5
A Country in Crisis..36

Map of Egypt 41
Timeline 42
Chapter Notes..43
Further Reading...44
Books..44
On the Internet..44
Works Consulted..44
Glossary 46
Index 47

CHAPTER 1

Coup!

On June 30, 2013, Tahrir Square in Egypt's capital city of Cairo was packed with uncounted thousands of people. They were demonstrating against the government of Mohamed Morsi, the country's first-ever democratically elected president. Chanting slogans, singing songs, and making speeches, the demonstrators demanded that Morsi quit as president.

Morsi, a member of an Islamist political party called the Muslim Brotherhood, had been in office for one year. During that time Egypt's economy had faltered, and shortages of electricity and fuel had occurred throughout the country. Morsi's opponents accused him of concentrating power in the hands of Islamists and failing to follow up on the hopes of the Revolution of 2011, which had toppled the dictatorial rule of longtime leader Hosni Mubarak.

Morsi made some controversial decisions during his year as president. He declared that the Egyptian courts could not review his decrees, he removed the country's prosecutor-general, and he pushed

This massive demonstration against President Morsi took place in front of the presidential palace in Cairo on June 30, 2013, the first anniversary of his term in office. Clashes between Morsi's opponents and his supporters led to at least seven deaths.

through a new constitution that gave him broad powers. As the country spiraled into chaos, tourism—a vital source of revenue for the Egyptian economy—declined. As a result, Morsi's actions became less and less acceptable to the country's citizens. Finally, in a repeat of the actions that led to Mubarak's ouster, millions of Egyptians throughout the country began demonstrating to demand his removal.

The big question for the demonstrators was what the Egyptian military would do. When the military had supported the protests against Mubarak, it virtually guaranteed that he would be forced out. If they did the same with the anti-Morsi protestors, it would mean trouble for the president. However, if they supported him and broke up the demonstrations, Morsi would likely be safe.

They didn't have to wait long.

The following day, the Egyptian armed forces issued a statement. "The national security of the state is exposed to extreme danger by the developments the nation is witnessing," it said. "The Armed Forces repeat their call for the people's demands to be met and give everyone 48 hours as a last chance

Born in 1951, Morsi lived in the United States for several years in the late 1970s and early 1980s. He received his PhD in engineering from the University of Southern California.

Because two of Morsi's five children were born in California while he was living there, they are legally US citizens.

to shoulder the burden of the historic moment that is happening in the nation."[1] The statement added that if those demands weren't met by the deadline, the military "will be obliged by its patriotic and historic responsibilities and by its respect for the demands of the great Egyptian people to announce a road map for the future."[2]

Morsi remained defiant, showing few signs that he was listening to the demonstrators who continued to pack Tahrir Square. Instead, he tried to stall for time. In a statement on his Facebook page, he offered to form an interim coalition government. He also proposed establishing an independent committee to handle and submit amendments for the controversial constitution.

The military rejected those offers. Egyptians were holding their breath as the last hours of the 48-hour deadline ticked away. What would happen to their country? Was Egypt about to descend into violence and chaos? Would there be fighting in the streets between pro- and anti-Morsi supporters?

It did not take long to find out what the first part of the "road map" included in the military statement involved. On July 4, 2013, a group of generals placed Morsi under house arrest. The first democratically elected president of Egypt had been overthrown by a military coup.

Shortly thereafter, General Abdel Fattah el-Sisi, the commander-in-chief of Egypt's armed forces, appeared on television. With

In Arabic, the word *tahrir* means "liberation."

military, religious, and political figures standing alongside him, el-Sisi announced that Morsi had been removed because he had not fulfilled "the hope for a national consensus."[3]

Throughout Egypt, the news was greeted with outrage by some and joy by others. Fighting erupted in several cities. Some people were killed.

What would happen to Egypt now? Was it about to slip into open warfare? Was the entire Middle East about to explode in the violence ignited by Egypt?

The world held its breath.

عاجل

بيان القيادة العامة للقوات المسلحة

Abdel Fattah el-Sisi, commander-in-chief of Egypt's armed forces, delivers a statement on July 3, 2013, about the "road map" for Egypt's governmental future, with specific dates for upcoming elections. He is flanked by religious, military, and government leaders.

Thousands of pro-Morsi demonstrators took to the streets of Cairo on August 23, 2013, nearly two months after his removal. Troops and armored vehicles were deployed to prevent violence.

CHAPTER 2

The Land of the Pharaohs

Egypt is one of the oldest and most famous countries in the world. Its very name conjures up the power of the pyramids, the majesty of its ancient civilization, the mystery of its mummies, and so much more. When civilizations were still emerging in other parts of the world, Egypt had been an advanced society for many centuries.

Egypt is defined by the Nile River. Most Egyptians, both in ancient times and today, live close to the Nile, as more than 95 percent of the country is primarily desert. The Nile is divided into two regions: the Delta and the Nile Valley. The Delta is a fan-shaped area in the northern part of the country, stretching along the coast of the Mediterranean Sea from Alexandria to the Suez Canal, and upriver to Cairo. The Nile Valley stretches roughly from Cairo south to the site of the modern-day Aswan Dam near the country's southern border.

Two different areas developed in ancient Egypt: Upper Egypt (primarily the Nile Valley) and Lower Egypt (primarily the Delta). Most historians agree

Map of Ancient Egypt

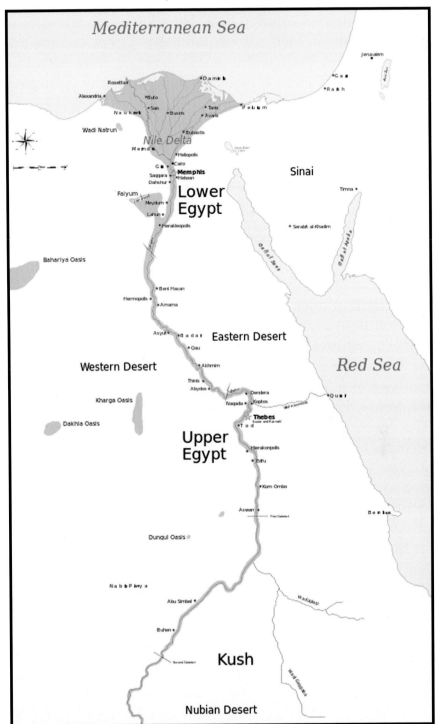

that Egypt's political and governmental history began about 3100 BCE (Before the Common Era). For a long time it was thought that a king named Menes from southern Egypt conquered the north and united both sections. However, it now seems more likely that "Menes" was actually named Narmer, who united the two sections peacefully.

Narmer and his successors became known by the title of pharaoh, which means "big house." Originally "pharaoh" referred to the royal palace, but eventually it came to mean the king as well.[1] The pharaoh was worshiped and obeyed as a god. He owned all the land in Egypt, and was entitled to whatever the land produced. The pharaoh could collect and redistribute whatever was grown on the land according to need or whim.

Thus the supreme authority of a central figure was established early in Egyptian history. The pharaoh controlled all political and economic institutions. The citizens became used to listening to one central figure without question.

Egypt's political/governmental system had an organized bureaucracy. The most important office was the vizier, the pharaoh's top advisor. The country was divided into provinces called nomes. Each nome had a leader called a gnomarch.

The development of an organized system of government and its accompanying bureaucracy led to an important advancement for Egypt (and ultimately the entire world). The government needed a way to keep records, so Egyptians developed a system of writing known as hieroglyphs. Hieroglyphs are symbols which represent objects and ideas. It seems likely that they originated at about the same time that Narmer united the two kingdoms.

For modern historians, the Egyptian system of record-keeping has another advantage. It allows them to divide Egypt's long history into several different periods. These periods are based on the ruling dynasties, or a series of pharaohs from the same family. However, the dates of each period are not exact. Rather, these dates are often approximations that help in understanding the sequence of events in the country's long history.

The first of these periods begins with Narmer and is known as the Late Predynastic Period. It lasted from about 3100 BCE to 2950 BCE. It was followed by the Early Dynastic Period (2950–2686 BCE), which in turn gave way to the Old Kingdom from 2686 to 2184 BCE. The famous Egyptian pyramids were built during this time as burial chambers for the pharaohs. The largest one, the Great Pyramid of Khufu, contains 2.3 million stone blocks, each of which weighs two and a half tons.[2]

The power of the pharaohs, and by extension the central government, began to crumble around 2350 BCE. Finally the country split in half, with a leading city in each half, much like the country had been previously. In Lower Egypt the city of Herakleopolis emerged; in Upper Egypt it was Thebes. This is known as the First Intermediate Period.

It was a time of lawlessness, trouble, and strife for Egypt. It did not end until 2055 BCE when Pharaoh Mentuhotep II of Thebes led a military campaign that conquered Herakleopolis. As historian Harry Adès notes, "[Mentuhotep's] actions allowed him to reunite Egypt, providing the platform for a long period of prosperity, artistic accomplishment and political unity."[3] Mentuhotep ruled for 50 years, and was responsible for increasing the size of Egypt's bureaucracy. He also created new government

The Great Pyramid of Khufu the oldest of the Seven Wonders of the ancient world and the only one still intact today.

Hieroglyphics was a system of writing developed to record governmental actions, and represents ancient Egypt in the minds of many people.

offices. His reign began the era known as the Middle Kingdom, which lasted until 1650 BCE. Once again the power of the pharaoh and the central government were dominant.

At the end of the Middle Kingdom Egypt again fell into a time of war and unrest called the Second Intermediate Period. This time it was due to the invasion of a group of people called the Hyksos. The Hyksos captured and occupied Lower Egypt, so again the country was divided. It wasn't until the military successes of a pharaoh named Ahmose that the Hyskos were driven out of Egypt and the country became whole again.

This reunification began the New Kingdom period, which lasted from 1550 to 1069 BCE. It was the Egypt of glory and legend, the nation whose invincible armies swept across the desert sands. One of the most noted figures is Ramses II, whose 67-year reign (1279–1212 BCE) is the second-longest in Egyptian history. "He was the pharaoh who made the name Ramses practically a synonym for Egyptian kingship," historian Barbara Mertz observes. "Ramses II's fame was created by the liberal use of a well-known principle of modern advertising—repetition."[4] Thousands of his images dotted Egypt to remind his subjects of his many accomplishments. Another is Tutankhamun (popularly known as King Tut), even though he ruled for only a few years (1331–1327 BCE) and died while still a teenager.

With the New Kingdom a strong central government was again established in Egypt. There were now two viziers, one for Upper Egypt and one for Lower Egypt. Again, as in times past, Egyptian government contained a vast bureaucracy. This time, however, the bureaucracy fell into three distinct categories: military, religious, and civil.

Like the ending of both the Old and Middle kingdoms, the final years of the New Kingdom were marked by an erosion in the authority of the pharaoh and a weakening of the central government. Although the king supposedly owned all of the land, in reality land was passed down from father to son. Thus rich families became more powerful, and the pharaoh, with less and less land to distribute, became weaker politically.

The Nubians—from a region south of Egypt—took advantage of the situation and conquered their neighbors to the north. That conquest began the Third Intermediate Period, which lasted from 1069 to 667 BCE.

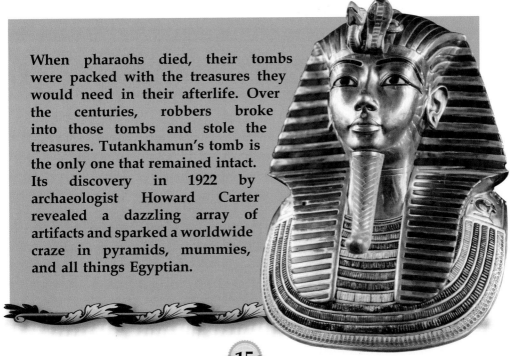

When pharaohs died, their tombs were packed with the treasures they would need in their afterlife. Over the centuries, robbers broke into those tombs and stole the treasures. Tutankhamun's tomb is the only one that remained intact. Its discovery in 1922 by archaeologist Howard Carter revealed a dazzling array of artifacts and sparked a worldwide craze in pyramids, mummies, and all things Egyptian.

There have been countless theories about how Tutankhamun died at age 19, including disease and assassination. In late 2013 a new theory suggested that his death was the result of being struck by a chariot—the ancient Egyptian equivalent of an automobile accident.

Another conqueror, the Assyrians, began what is known as the Late Period when they seized control in 667 BCE. About a century and a half later the Persians supplanted them. The Egyptians were not pleased being under Persian rule, so when Alexander the Great from Macedonia (a state in northern Greece) entered Egypt with his army in 332, he was hailed as a liberator. He took the country without a struggle and brought the Late Period to an end. Alexander's direct rule over Egypt was relatively short—he died in 323 BCE—but significant. He founded the city of Alexandria on the coast of the Mediterranean Sea. It would grow to become one of the world's major cities during antiquity.

Alexander's death caused his empire to be divided among his generals. Ptolemy, a friend of Alexander's since childhood, wound up with Egypt. Ptolemy and his descendants ruled Egypt as the Ptolemaic Dynasty. They developed an elaborate governmental system that began with the pharaoh and stretched all the way down to the village level. The main reason for establishing this system was to maximize revenues.[5] Such items as glassware and textiles were strictly limited to government-sponsored monopolies to produce, which meant that the government could keep tight control over the taxes such production generated. Private businesses were also tightly controlled and taxed by the government.

Pepi II, the last pharaoh of the Old Kingdom, is credited with a 94-year reign, the longest in world history.

The Alexandria Lighthouse was another of the Seven Wonders of the ancient world. It was destroyed by a series of earthquakes between 956 and 1323.

The last ruler of the Ptolemic Dynasty was the legendary Cleopatra, who reigned from 51 to 30 BCE. By this time Rome was rising as a power in the world, and Cleopatra knew that it was only a matter of time until Egypt would be swallowed up during Rome's expansion and lose its independence. To avoid this, she tried to make alliances with Roman leaders. At first she tried Julius Caesar, but his murder in 44 BCE forced her to seek a new protector. She and Mark Antony, one of three Romans who shared power after Caesar's murder, became lovers. They had three children and lived in Alexandria. However, their forces were defeated by their Roman rival Octavian in 31 BCE at the Battle of Actium. The following year, with Octavian closing in, Antony killed himself. Cleopatra committed suicide soon afterward, possibly by allowing herself to be bitten by a cobra.

Cleopatra's death brought the long line of pharaohs to an end. It would take nearly 2,000 years for Egypt to regain its political independence.

CHAPTER 3

Struggle for Independence

Once Egypt became a part of the Roman Empire, the once-mighty nation entered a long period in which it was subservient to several different empires. The Roman emperors ruled Egypt as divine kings, much like the previous rulers, and largely kept intact the old Ptolemaic system.[1] Beneath the emperor in the governmental hierarchy were four regional governors. Below them were 30 other officials who each ruled one of the nomes. The duties of the officials in the extensive governmental bureaucracy set up to support this system were, according to a philosopher named Philo, "intricate and diversified, hardly grasped even by those who have made a business of studying them from their earliest years."[2]

Egyptian towns and villages were at the bottom of this governmental system. Although there was no real self-government, the towns were responsible for things such as the maintenance of public works, tax collection, and the delivery of the harvest to governmental storage areas. A few local officials oversaw things.

The Roman Emperor Diocletian strengthened Egypt's governmental structure and made it easier to manage.

DIOCLETIANVS

In the third century CE (Common Era) the vast Roman Empire began to suffer from invasions by outside groups, economic instability, and lawlessness and unrest. Eventually the empire was split into two sections — east and west. Egypt was part of the eastern section, which later became known as the Byzantine Empire. Near the end of the third century, the Emperor Diocletian attempted to strengthen the Egyptian governmental structure. He broke the administrative units into smaller units that were easier to supervise. He also replaced the nomes, which had existed for thousands of years, with six separate provinces.

In 603, tensions between the Byzantines and the neighboring Sasanian Empire — which encompassed much of the same territory as the old Persian Empire — erupted into full-scale warfare. About 619, the Sasanians occupied Egypt, though they soon withdrew and the country reverted to the Byzantines. However, a new threat was emerging.

This time the challenge came from Arabia in the form of a new religion, Islam, which was founded by the Prophet Muhammad early in the 600s. Muslim armies entered northern Egypt in late 639, and within three years the country was theirs.

The soldiers, many of whom had been born and raised in harsh desert conditions in Arabia, were amazed at Alexandria. Their leader, Amr ibn al-As, wrote, "It is impossible for me to describe the variety of its riches and beauty; I shall content myself by saying that it contains 4000 palaces, 4000 baths, 400 theatres or places of amusement, and 12,000 grocers."[3]

The Muslims brought significant changes to Egyptian politics and government. They did not rule the country from Alexandria. Instead, they created a completely new capital city called Fustat. The ruler of Egypt was not a pharaoh or king but a governor who was appointed by the Muslim leader, or caliph, who resided in Baghdad in modern-day Iraq.

In 868 Ahmed ibn Tulun became ruler of Egypt. Through taxation reform and improvements to the country's agricultural system, he became so popular that he actually governed Egypt independently of the caliph. However, his death in 884 and the murder of his son Khumarawayh sent Egypt spinning into chaos. The rulers in Baghdad put tighter controls on Egypt and installed

The Ibn Tulun Mosque in Cairo was commissioned by Egyptian governor Ahmed ibn Tulun, who implemented taxation and agricultural reforms. The mosque was completed in 879.

a series of military governors. However, this system did not work well; the vast governmental bureaucracy and administrative system that was in place functioned erratically without a strong ruler at the helm.

Politically, however, help was coming for Egypt in the form of two great ruling dynasties. First was the Fatimid Dynasty, which ruled Egypt from 969 to 1171. The Fatimids founded a new capital city not far from Fustat named al-Qahirah, which eventually became known as Cairo. Once again, a strong figure was at the head of the Egyptian government—the caliph. Flowing down from him was a vast administrative and governmental bureaucracy headed by the caliph's chief aide, the vizier. The Fatimid caliphs undertook an extensive building program throughout the country, maintained the waterworks, reduced taxes, and increased agricultural yield, which helped build Egypt into a rich trading country.

The Fatimids were succeeded by the Ayyubid Dynasty, founded by the great Muslim leader Saladin in 1171. He took the title of "sultan," an Arabic word that means "strength" or "authority," and the term passed down to his successors. As great an administrator as he was a military genius, Saladin encouraged education, supported the arts, and kept Egypt at the forefront of trading nations.

The Ayyubid dynasty relied on warriors from Turkey called Mamluks to populate the army. Slave traders would buy young boys and take them to Egypt. There they would be purchased by the head of a Mamluk family to join his household and be trained in the art of warfare.

When the slave completed his training he was let go to enter the army, but most stayed loyal to their families. Mamluks

The Fatimids claimed that they were the direct descendants of the Prophet Muhammad's daughter Fatima.

Saladin was one of the greatest of all Egyptian leaders and founder of the Ayyubid Dynasty. This image was created by Gustave Doré (1832–1883).

counted on their patrons' assistance for career advancement. By the same token, the patron's reputation and power depended on his recruits.

The Mamluks became so powerful that in 1250 they overthrew the Ayyubids and brought a massive change to the government and politics of Egypt. The system they established did not rely on heredity, in which a father passed down land or political office to his son. Rather, it rewarded the strongest and best fighters.

What this meant was that nothing in Egypt was given to someone who was not a strong fighter. Politically, this completely changed things, since when a sultan died the new one was the strongest militarily. The governors of Egypt who ruled the outlying provinces were loyal to their patrons, so the practice of an unfit child or relative becoming a ruler was eliminated. Loyalty was constantly refreshed with each generation.

The Mamluks were fearsome warriors who governed Egypt. Here they capture the city of Tripoli (in modern-day Lebanon) from the Crusaders in 1289.

In 1517 the Ottoman Empire, centered in modern-day Turkey, conquered Egypt and ended the reign of the Mamluks. The Ottomans ruled from their capital city of Istanbul and kept the Mamluks in power in Egypt to run the country for them. Thus the Ottoman influence was never widely felt in Egyptian politics and government, although Turkish did become the language of the Egyptian ruling class. Egypt became increasingly a backwater, plagued by neglect and excessive taxation. Its economy was in shambles.

That situation began changing with the invasion of the country by France's Napoleon Bonaparte, who landed at Alexandria—which was just a shadow of its former glory—with over 30,000 troops in July 1798. France was at war with Great Britain. Napoleon's intention was to cut off communications with India, the most valuable British colony, by seizing Egypt.

Napoleon brought with him scholars, scientists, and artists, whose intention was to study Egypt. The information they compiled about Egypt's ancient culture—the pyramids, Sphinx, and so on—ignited the fascination with Egypt that continues today. The discovery of the Rosetta Stone in 1799 by a group of French soldiers rebuilding a fort near the town of Rosetta is considered one of the greatest archaeological discoveries in history.

The Rosetta Stone has the same inscription written in three languages: hieroglyphic (the language of important religious and official documents), demotic (the common language of Egypt), and ancient Greek (the language of Egypt's Ptolemaic rulers at the time the inscriptions were made). No one could translate hieroglyphics or demotic. But scholars were familiar

The carving on the Rosetta Stone dates back to 196 BCE. Today it is in the British Museum in London, where it is the most-visited single exhibit.

Napoleon leads members of his staff during his invasion of Egypt. The artist is Jean-Léon Gérôme (1824–1904).

with ancient Greek. That familiarity enabled them to translate the other two and read the vast array of ancient hieroglyphic records.

The French occupation of Egypt lasted only until 1801. Although brief, it severely damaged the Mamluks' power and made them ripe for overthrow.

CHAPTER 4

From Tyranny to Democracy to . . . ?

Muhammad Ali was named viceroy, or pasha, of Egypt in 1805. He was supposedly ruling the country on behalf of the Ottomans, but their empire was declining and they continued to largely ignore Egypt. Thus Ali ruled Egypt virtually as an independent country.

Ali was a fearsome warrior. He defeated a British force in 1807, decorating the streets of Cairo with the severed heads of the dead soldiers mounted on spikes. He dealt with the Mamluks in the same brutal manner. In March 1811, Ali held a celebration in Cairo and invited nearly 500 of the top Mamluks. At the conclusion of the festivities the gates were closed, trapping the Mamluks. Sharpshooters suddenly appeared and killed hundreds of Mamluks as they tried to flee. After the gunfire ended, Ali's soldiers rushed in with swords and axes and killed any survivors. According to legend, only one escaped.[1]

The defeat of the Mamluks removed them from Egypt's political scene. Ali began to modernize

Painting of Muhammad Ali in 1840 by French artist Auguste Couder (1805–1848)

Egypt. Factories were built for making textiles, munitions, and numerous other products. Ali developed a modern army and navy, launched a vast public works program, and improved public education. He also improved irrigation. He formed "deliberative councils," which made suggestions that Ali often turned into laws and governmental policies. He also re-established a top-down governmental bureaucracy, with seven major departments that were further broken down into bureaus and workshops.

The ultimate modernization project for Egypt was the digging of the Suez Canal, which began in 1859. By the time the canal

Construction of the Suez Canal was undertaken by France's Ferdinand de Lesseps to connect the Mediterranean Sea with the Red Sea. This engraving was made shortly before its completion in 1869.

was completed ten years later, the Egyptian pasha was Ismail, Ali's grandson. Ismail enjoyed a lavish lifestyle; he also launched vast building projects throughout Egypt to continue Ali's modernization efforts. To finance these ventures he took loans from Great Britain and France, which he was unable to pay back. Thus, even though Egypt was still officially part of the Ottoman Empire, it was easy for Britain (at the time the most powerful nation on earth) to have the Ottomans force Ismail out of power in 1879.

Internal instability and a rise of nationalism followed Ismail's departure, which resulted in Britain occupying Egypt in 1882 to protect European interests. Although the country was still technically under the sultan's control, Great Britain now made all of the important political decisions. As Harry Adès notes, "Ismail had intended to liberate Egypt from the ignorance, squalor and poverty of its medieval past; but in the process of funding its passage to modernity he had thrown the country into the shackles of foreign control."[2]

The British occupation was supposed to be brief. However, within a year after Lord Cromer was appointed as consul general of Egypt, he decided that Egyptians were incapable of governing themselves.[3] That belief, and the fact that the country was in shambles internally — a bloated bureaucracy, a poor infrastructure, and massive debt — made the British occupation last much longer. The British installed "advisers" for each of the Egyptian ministers. These advisers actually ran the government; the ministers soon learned that failing to follow an adviser's advice would mean the loss of their job.[4]

When World War I erupted in 1914 and the Ottoman Empire joined with Germany against Great Britain and its allies, it ended the years of the English and the Turks working together in Egypt. The British declared Egypt a protectorate, which made it a British colony. The Egyptians resented British rule. After the war ended, Egyptian feelings for independence ran high. A new political party called the Wafd pushed for independence, and Great Britain knew that it could not keep Egypt as a protectorate. Yet the British wanted to make certain that the vital Suez Canal remained

Defending the Suez Canal against a possible Ottoman invasion in World War I was a high priority for the British. The troops in this 1916 photo are awaiting orders.

open. So in 1923 Britain imposed a constitutional monarchy in Egypt, meaning that a king was the head of the government. At the same time, a new constitution established a parliament that consisted of a Senate and Chamber of Deputies. This constitutional monarchy came with numerous conditions that kept Britain as a key player in Egyptian affairs, particularly in assuring continued operation of the Suez Canal.

This latest evolution in Egyptian government and politics pleased no one. New political parties formed in Egypt, such as the Muslim Brotherhood—an Islamic fundamentalist party—in 1928. For years the Egyptian political scene was filled with chaos and confusion. The situation came to a head in 1952 when King Farouk appointed four different cabinets, trying desperately to find the right combination to govern effectively.

In July that year, a group of military officers led by Colonel Gamal Abdel Nasser who called themselves the Free Officers staged a coup that toppled Farouk. This coup injected the military into Egyptian politics, a situation that continues today.

Over the next few years Nasser consolidated his power.

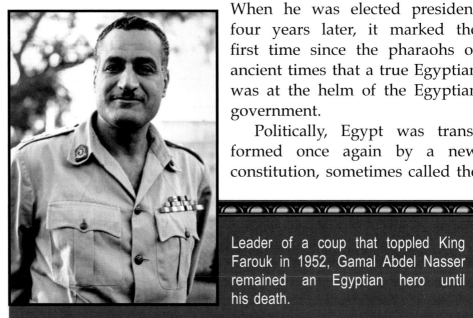

When he was elected president four years later, it marked the first time since the pharaohs of ancient times that a true Egyptian was at the helm of the Egyptian government.

Politically, Egypt was transformed once again by a new constitution, sometimes called the

Leader of a coup that toppled King Farouk in 1952, Gamal Abdel Nasser remained an Egyptian hero until his death.

When King Farouk was deposed, Egypt technically remained a monarchy with Farouk's baby son Ahmed Faud as king. The following year the monarchy was abolished when the country became a republic.

1956 Constitution. Although the constitution established an assembly of representatives, the assembly could not originate or pass laws; its primary function was to consult with the president and other officials. The new constitution also banned all political parties except the state-controlled National Unity Party. All power resided in the hands of Nasser.

He used this power to nationalize the Suez Canal Company that same year. Revenue from ships passing through the canal went to the government of Egypt rather than the owners of the company, which included the British and French governments. In response, Britain, France, and Israel attacked Egypt and took control of the canal. The United States and the Soviet Union pressured Britain and France to return the canal to Egypt. Nasser became a hero for standing up to the western countries.

Egyptians in Port Said, located at the northern end of the Suez Canal, clear debris after the 1956 Suez Crisis. Despite the destruction, the crisis helped boost Nasser's popularity.

In 1958 Egyptian politics evolved further with the creation of the United Arab Republic (UAR)—a combination of Egypt, Syria, and (for a short time) Yemen. The UAR dissolved in 1961, but Nasser continued ruling Egypt. Despite military defeats—most notably in the Six-Day War in 1967, an overwhelming victory by neighboring Israel—a souring economy, and bad relations with Western countries such as the United States, Nasser remained president of Egypt until dying of a heart attack in September, 1970. He remains an Egyptian hero.

Nasser was succeeded by his vice-president, Anwar Sadat. Sadat repaired relations with the West. Politically, Sadat caused a major stir by signing a peace treaty with Israel that recognized Israel's right to exist. This treaty caused Egypt to be isolated in the Arab world and made Sadat a traitor in the eyes of many Arabs.

Egyptian President Anwar Sadat and Israeli Prime Minister Menachem Begin join hands with US President Jimmy Carter in March 1979 at the White House. Carter negotiated a peace treaty between the longtime enemies.

Hosni Mubarak was the commander of the Egyptian Air Force from 1972 to 1975.

In 1971 the Egyptian government evolved once again with the passage of a new constitution. The document called the country a republic with a democratic, socialist system. There was one lawmaking assembly, the 454-member People's Assembly. There was also a 210-member Shura Council, which reviewed legislation passed by the Assembly. The president served as head of state, and he appointed the prime minister.

Sadat was assassinated by Islamic extremists on October 6, 1981. His vice-president, Hosni Mubarak, who had been sitting next to him when he was shot, took over as president. Mubarak immediately put the country under martial law, where it remained for his entire term in power. The government maintained that it was necessary to fight Islamic terrorism. All religious-based political parties, including the Muslim Brotherhood, were banned from having their members serve in the People's Assembly. The primary political party was the government-backed and controlled National Democratic Party.

Mubarak ruled Egypt with an iron grip until early 2011, when protests began occurring throughout the country. These protests were sparked by concerns over rising unemployment, a faltering economy, and a decline in the value of Egyptian currency. In addition, Mubarak had never named a vice-president, and there was concern that the aging president was preparing to name his son Gamal as his successor.

On January 25, 2011, an especially large anti-Mubarak protest was held in Cairo. Security forces tried to break up the demonstrators, but the protests spread throughout Egypt. The protestors demanded that Egypt institute democracy. On January 29, trying to appease the protestors, Mubarak named Omar Suleiman vice-president. When that didn't quiet them, a few days

President Hosni Mubarak resigned after 30 years in office.

later he announced that he would not run for re-election later that year. When that still didn't do the trick, on February 10 Mubarak announced that he was handing over his powers to the vice-president but would remain as president. The following day, however, Vice-President Suleiman announced that Mubarak was stepping down. A month later, the Supreme Council of the Armed Forces of Egypt adopted the Constitutional Declaration of 2011,

Hosni Mubarak's nearly 30-year rule was the longest since Muhammad Ali (1805–1848).

Protesters packing Tahrir Square in Cairo pause for prayers on February 1, 2011, the eighth day of demonstrations against Mubarak.

which was intended to pave the way for a new constitution to replace the one established 40 years earlier.

Later that year, the once-banned Muslim Brotherhood re-emerged as a potent political force when they won nearly half the seats in voting for a new parliament. In June 2012, Morsi won Egypt's first-ever democratic presidential election, with 51.7 percent of the vote. However, once in office Morsi made several moves—including yet another constitution—aimed at giving him greater powers. Not long afterward, he was gone.

CHAPTER 5
A Country in Crisis

After President Morsi was deposed, the country was rocked by demonstrations, some in support of him, others favoring the military that overthrew him.

When it took over, the military announced a "road map" for Egypt's political future. It included the suspension of the Constitution that had been adopted the previous year, the formation of a national reconciliation committee, and another round of elections for president and parliament.

Demonstrations continued over the next few months. As time went on, several youth groups that initially supported Morsi's overthrow and had been among the key figures in forcing out Mubarak began turning against the military-backed government. One reason was the government's passage of a harsh new law in November 2013 that sought to stop protests and dissent, which they said was hurting Egypt's economy.

In December 2013 the military government used the new law to sentence three of the country's most prominent youth activists to prison terms for throwing rocks at police. The law has been criticized as harsher than any passed during former president Mubarak's tenure, and as a way to stifle dissent of any type.

A few days later, the government declared the Muslim Brotherhood political party to be a terrorist organization. It said that holding a leadership position in the group could be grounds for the death penalty. Calling the group a terrorist organization was something that had never been done before, even during the years that the party had been banned. The terror designation meant that any member of the Muslim Brotherhood could be arrested just for belonging to the party.

In January 2014, Egyptian voters approved a new constitution based on the 1971 version. It "strengthens the country's three key institutions—the military, the police and the judiciary," notes journalist Patrick Kingsley. "It also gives more rights to women

In January 2014, Egyptians voted on yet another new constitution, this one to replace the one passed under deposed President Morsi.

and disabled people, and removes certain Islamist-leaning clauses inserted under Morsi, while maintaining the principles of Islamic sharia as the main source of legislation."[1] According to the government, over 20 million voters approved the new constitution. This figure represented 98.1 percent of the people who went to the polls.

However, concerns were raised about the fairness of the voting. There had been no public debate of the new constitution before the vote, and Egyptian police arrested anyone who campaigned against the proposed constitution. In addition, just 38 percent of eligible voters actually went to the polls.

One reason for the low turnout was that members of the Muslim Brotherhood boycotted the election. They quickly challenged the results. "Even if 38 percent of the voters took part, that still means that 62 percent of the public rejects [the military government]," said a member of a coalition representing the Muslim Brotherhood. "They are trying to legitimize their coup."[2]

Supporters of the Muslim Brotherhood hold a public protest in January 2014, even though the government had declared several weeks earlier that the organization was a terrorist group and demonstrations such as this one were illegal.

In 2014, Hosni Mubarak and his two sons were sentenced to jail terms on corruption charges.

US Secretary of State John Kerry also raised concerns. He called on the Egyptian government to live up to the pledge it made when the coup first occurred to respect and expand rights while bringing the country to a civilian-led government by way of free and fair elections. "Democracy is more than any one referendum or election,"[3] he said.

A political analyst from Cairo's American University said, "This [the 98.1 percent 'yes' vote] is a very alarming figure [in a country as complex as Egypt]. Something has gone very wrong."[4]

On the other hand, the new constitution appealed to many people who feel that it offered stability after several years of chaos. "I'm saying yes so that the country can rise again, and so that the people can eat,"[5] said Salah Abdel Hamid, a 63-year-old Cairo shopkeeper.

The new constitution calls for a president, who can be elected to two four-year terms. The constitution also establishes a parliament with at least 450 members, though this number probably will exceed 600. It's likely that there will be plenty of candidates for those seats. As of January 2014, the CIA World Factbook listed 16 political parties in Egypt, though parties based on religion, race, geography, or gender are banned. Islam is the official state religion. The Minister of Defense can be appointed by the military for the next eight years.

Some people are concerned about the manner in which the judiciary—besides the president and parliament, the third branch of the Egyptian government—was strengthened by the new constitution. As *Daily News Egypt* points out, it "gives absolute power to the Supreme Constitutional Court [Egypt's highest court] in choosing its members, making it the first constitutional court in the world that has this kind of authority."[6] Previously members had been chosen by the president.

Abdel Fattah el-Sisi had a 37-year career in the Egyptian army before resigning in 2014 to run for president.

As had been widely expected, Abdel Fattah el-Sisi easily won the presidential election in late May, polling nearly 97 percent of the votes. "It is now time to work—work that will carry Egypt to a bright tomorrow and better future and restore stability," he said. "The future is a white page and it is in our hands to fill it as we wish."[7]

But as had been the case with the vote for the constitution four months earlier, his victory was characterized by a relatively low voter turnout. So as Egyptians looked ahead, they were confronted by a number of questions. Would their country continue to be torn apart by riots and protests? Would the Egyptian economy recover and tourists return? Would el-Sisi become a dictatorial leader or someone who leads Egypt to democracy?

Too many questions, and too few answers. Egypt remains turbulent and faces an uncertain future.

In June 2014 former armed forces commander-in-chief Abdel Fattah el-Sisi was sworn in as Egypt's new president in front of members of the Supreme Constitutional Court.

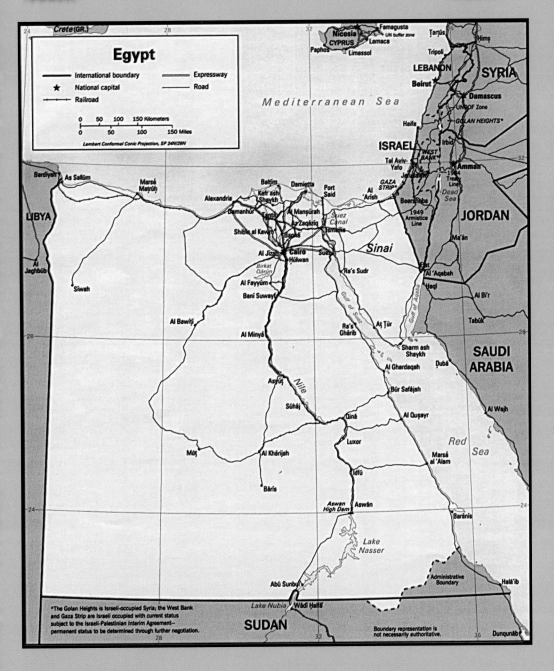

TIMELINE

Dates BCE

3100	Narmer, a.k.a Menes, unifies Upper and Lower Egypt; the term "pharaoh" begins to be used for the Egyptian ruler.
2686–2184	The Old Kingdom.
2055–1650	The Middle Kingdom.
1550–1069	The New Kingdom.
667	The Assyrians conquer Egypt.
332	Alexander the Great conquers Egypt.
323	The Ptolemic Dynasty begins its reign in Egypt.
51	Cleopatra becomes pharaoh.
30	Roman forces defeat Cleopatra, who commits suicide, and Egypt becomes part of the Roman Empire.

Dates CE

4th century	Egypt becomes part of the Byzantine Empire.
619	Persia occupies Egypt.
642	Muslim forces take control of Egypt.
969	Egypt is ruled by the Fatimid Dynasty.
1171	Egypt becomes part of the Ayyubid Dynasty.
1250	The Mamluks take control of Egypt.
1517	Egypt becomes part of the Ottoman Empire.
1798	Napoleon Bonaparte invades Egypt.
1805	Muhammad Ali assumes control of Egypt.
1882	Great Britain occupies Egypt, although it remains a part of the Ottoman Empire.
1914	Great Britain makes Egypt a protectorate.
1923	Egypt becomes a constitutional monarchy.
1928	The Muslim Brotherhood political party forms in Egypt.
1952	King Farouk is overthrown by the Free Officers.
1953	Egypt becomes a republic.
1958	Egypt becomes part of the United Arab Republic.
1970	Anwar al-Sadat becomes president.
1971	A new constitution labels Egypt a republic with a socialist system.
1981	Sadat is assassinated and succeeded by Hosni Mubarak.
2011	Mubarak steps down.
2012	Mohamed Morsi of the Muslim Brotherhood becomes Egypt's first democratically elected president.
2013	Morsi is overthrown in a military coup.
2014	General Abdel Fattah el-Sisi wins presidential election.

CHAPTER NOTES

Chapter 1. Coup!

1. Text of Egyptian Military Ultimatum. Associated Press, July 1, 2013. http://bigstory.ap.org/article/text-egyptian-military-ultimatum

2. Ibid.

3. David D. Kirkpatrick, "Army Ousts Egypt's President; Morsi Is Taken into Military Custody." *The New York Times*, July 5, 2013. http://www.nytimes.com/2013/07/04/world/middleeast/egypt.html?pagewanted=all

Chapter 2. The Land of the Pharaohs

1. Jason Thompson, *A History of Egypt* (New York: Anchor Books, 2008), p. 26.

2. Harry Adès, *A Traveller's History of Egypt* (Northampton, MA: Interlink Books, 2007), pp. 50–51.

3. Ibid., p. 63.

4. Barbara Mertz, *Temples, Tombs & Hieroglyphs: A Popular History of Ancient Egypt*. Second Edition (New York: William Morrow, 2007), p. 245.

5. Thompson, *History of Egypt*, p. 104.

Chapter 3. Struggle for Independence

1. Jason Thompson, *A History of Egypt* (New York: Anchor Books, 2008), p. 104.

2. Ibid., p. 124.

3. Harry Adès, *A Traveller's History of Egypt* (Northampton, MA: Interlink Books, 2007), p. 203.

Chapter 4. From Tyranny to Democracy to ...?

1. Matthew D. Firestone, Michael Benanav, Thomas Hall, Anthony Sattin, *Egypt* (Oakland, CA: Lonely Planet, 2010), p. 40.

2. Harry Adès, *A Traveller's History of Egypt* (Northampton, MA: Interlink Books, 2007), p. 285.

3. Jason Thompson, *A History of Egypt* (New York: Anchor Books, 2008), p. 254.

4. Ibid, p. 255.

Chapter 5. A Country in Crisis

1. Patrick Kingsley, "Egypt's new constitution gets 98% 'yes' vote." *The Guardian*, January 18, 2014. http://www.theguardian.com/world/2014/jan/18/egypt-constitution-yes-vote-mohamed-morsi

2. Mariam Rizk, "Voters overwhelmingly back new Egypt Constitution." Associated Press, January 19, 2014. http://bigstory.ap.org/article/egypt-death-toll-friday-violence-rises-4

3. Ibid.

4. Hamza Hendawi, "Analysis: Egypt vote muddles political outlook." Associated Press, January 19, 2014. http://news.yahoo.com/analysis-egypt-vote-muddles-political-outlook-192616441.html

5. Kingsley, "Egypt's new constitution."

6. "The 2014 Egyptian Constitution: Without accountability, checks or balances: Part II." *Daily News Egypt*, March 25, 2014. http://www.dailynewsegypt.com/2014/03/25/2014-egyptian-constitution-without-accountability-checks-balances-part-ii/

7. Maggie Michael, "Abdel Fattah El Sissi Officially Wins Egyptian Presidential Election." Associated Press, June 3, 2004. http://www.huffingtonpost.com/2014/06/03/sissi-egypt-election_n_5439218.html

FURTHER READING

Books

Adamson, Heather. *Ancient Egypt: An Interactive History Adventure*. North Mankato, MN: You Choose Books, 2009.

Blackaby, Susan. *Cleopatra: Egypt's Last and Greatest Queen*. New York: Sterling Publishing, 2009.

Boyer, Crispin. *National Geographic Kids Everything Ancient Egypt: Dig Into A Treasure Trove of Facts, Photos and Fun*. Washington, DC: National Geographic Children's Books, 2012.

Green, Roger Lancelyn. *Tales of Ancient Egypt*. London: Puffin Classics, 2011.

Gutner, Howard. *Egypt*. New York: Children's Press, 2009.

Williams, Marcia. *Ancient Egypt: Tales of Gods and Pharaohs*. Somerville, MA: Candlewick Press, 2013.

On the Internet

Egypt. The CIA World Factbook.
  https://www.cia.gov/library/publications/the-world-factbook/geos/eg.html

Egypt Travel: Egypt's Official Tourism Website.
  http://www.egypt.travel/

Egypt. Infoplease.com
  http://www.infoplease.com/country/egypt.html

US Relations with Egypt. US Department of State.
  http://www.state.gov/r/pa/ei/bgn/5309.htm

History of Egypt. Lonely Planet.
  http://www.lonelyplanet.com/egypt/history

Works Consulted

"The 2014 Egyptian Constitution: Without accountability, checks or balances: Part II." *Daily News Egypt*, March 25, 2014. http://www.dailynewsegypt.com/2014/03/25/2014-egyptian-constitution-without-accountability-checks-balances-part-ii/

Adès, Harry. *A Traveller's History of Egypt*. Northampton, MA: Interlink Books, 2007.

Baer, Gabriel. *Studies in the Social History of Modern Egypt*. Chicago: The University of Chicago Press, 1969.

Bentley, John J. IV. *Egypt Guide*. Cold Spring Harbor, NY: Open Road Publishing, 1998.

El Deeb, Sarah, and Mariam Rizk. "Icons of Egypt's protest movement sentenced to three years in prison." Associated Press, December 23, 2013. http://bigstory.ap.org/article/egypt-activists-get-3-years-prison-protest

Firestone, Matthew D., Michael Benanav, Thomas Hall, and Anthony Sattin. *Egypt*. Oakland, CA: Lonely Planet, 2010.

Hendawi, Hamza. "Analysis: Egypt vote muddles political outlook." Yahoo! News, January 20, 2014. http://news.yahoo.com/analysis-egypt-vote-muddles-politicaloutlook-192616441.html

Hendawi, Hamza, Sarah el Deeb and Maggie Michael. "Egypt's military gives Morsi 48-hour ultimatum." Yahoo! News, July 1, 2013. http://news.yahoo.com/egypts-military-gives-morsi-48-hour-ultimatum-230415249.html

FURTHER READING

"Key events in Egypt's revolution and transition leading up to referendum on draft constitution," Fox News. http://www.foxnews.com/world/2012/12/21/key-events-in-egypt-revolution-and-transition-leading-up-to-referendum-on-draft-constitution

Kingsley, Patrick. "Egypt's new constitution gets 98% 'yes' vote." *The Guardian*, January 18, 2014. http://www.theguardian.com/world/2014/jan/18/egypt-constitution-yes-vote-mohamed-morsi

Kirkpatrick, David D. "Army Ousts Egypt's President; Morsi Is Taken Into Military Custody." *The New York Times*, July 5, 2013. http://www.nytimes.com/2013/07/04/world/middleeast/egypt.html?pagewanted=all

Kirkpatrick, David D., "Overwhelming Vote for Egypt's Constitution Raises Concern." *The New York Times*, January 18, 2014. http://www.nytimes.com/2014/01/19/world/middleeast/vote-validates-egypts-constitution-and-military-takeover.html

Mertz, Barbara. *Temples, Tombs & Hieroglyphs: A Popular History of Ancient Egypt*. Second Edition. New York: William Morrow, 2007.

Michael, Maggie. "Abdel Fattah El Sissi Officially Wins Egyptian Presidential Election." Associated Press, June 3, 2004. http://www.huffingtonpost.com/2014/06/03/sissi-egypt-election_n_5439218.html

Michael, Maggie. "Egypt hikes assault on Muslim Brotherhood." Associated Press, December 26, 2013. http://www.denverpost.com/restaurants/ci_24795043/explosion-hits-bus-egyptian-capital-wounding-5

Michael, Maggie. "Official: Egyptian voters have backed new charter." Yahoo! News, January 16, 2014. http://news.yahoo.com/official-egyptian-voters-backed-charter-100856281.html

Posener, Georges. *Dictionary of Egyptian Civilization*. New York: Tudor Publishing, 1959.

"President Morsi Overthrown in Egypt." Aljazeera.com, July 4, 2013. http://www.aljazeera.com/news/middleeast/2013/07/20137319828176718.html

Rizk, Mariam. "Voters overwhelmingly back new Egypt Constitution." Associated Press, January 19, 2014. http://bigstory.ap.org/article/egypt-death-toll-friday-violence-rises-4

Text of Egyptian Military Ultimatum. Associated Press, July 1, 2013. http://bigstory.ap.org/article/text-egyptian-military-ultimatum

Thompson, Jason. *A History of Egypt*. New York: Anchor Books, 2008.

Vatikiotis, P.J. *The History of Egypt*. Baltimore, MD: The Johns Hopkins University Press, 1980.

Waterfield, Gordon. *Egypt*. New York: Walker and Company, 1967.

GLOSSARY

chaos (KAY-ahss) — Utter confusion or disorder.

conjure (KAHN-juhr) — Make something appear.

consensus (kuhn-SEN-suhss) — General agreement.

consolidate (kuhn-SAHL-uh-deyt) — Combine several elements into
a stronger whole.

controversy (KAHN-truh-vur-see — Public dispute or argument.

coup (KOO) — A sudden, often violent takeover of a government.

decree (dee-KREE) — A formal order, especially one having the
force of law.

defiant (dee-FIE-uhnt) — Boldly resistant or challenging.

dissent (dih-SENT) — Disagreement with the goals or methods
of a government.

equivalent (ee-KWI-vuh-luhnt) — Equal in value.

erratic (eh-RAT-ik) — Unpredictable, wandering, irregular.

falter (FAWL-tuhr) — To hesitate; begin to lose momentum.

hierarchy (HIE-uhr-ahr-kee) — A system in which people or things
are ranked one above another.

intact (in-TAKT) — Unbroken, whole.

interim (IN-ter-uhm) — Temporary.

Islamist (iss-LAHM-ist) — A movement that seeks to impose the
values of the religion of Islam in all areas of life.

liberator (LIB-uh-ray-tuhr) — One who frees someone or
something.

martial law (MAHR-shull LAW) — Control of an area by military
forces and the suspension of ordinary laws.

spiral (SPY-ruhl) — Winding in a continuous curve.

stifle (STY-fuhl) — To suppress or restrain.

strife (STRYF) — A struggle or clash.

teeter (TEE-tuhr) — Move unsteadily; sway back and forth.

INDEX

Actium, Battle of   17
Ahmose   14
Alexandria   10, 16, 17, 20, 24
Alexander the Great   16
Ali, Muhammad   26, 27
Antony, Mark   17
Assyrians   16
Ayyubid Dynasty   21, 22, 23
Bonaparte, Napoleon   24
Caesar, Julius   17
Cairo   4, 10, 21, 26, 33
Carter, Howard   15
Cleopatra   17
Delta   10
Diocletian   19
Early Dynastic Period   13
el-Sisi, Abdel Fattah   7, 8, 40
Farouk, King   30, 31
Faud, Ahmed   31
Fatamid Dynasty   21
First Intermediate Period   13
Great Pyramid of Khufu   13
Herakleopolis   13
hieroglyphs   12
Hyksos   14
Ibn Tulun, Ahmed   20
Ismail   28
Israel   31, 32
Kerry, John   39
Khumarawayh   20
Late Period   16
Late Predynastic Period   16
Lighthouse of Alexandria   17
Lord Cromer   28
Mamluks   21, 23, 25, 26
Menes   12
Mentuhotep   13, 14
Middle Kingdom   14, 15

Morsi, Mohamed   4, 5, 6, 8, 35, 36, 38
Mubarak, Hosni   4, 5, 6, 7, 33, 34, 36, 37, 39
Muslim Brotherhood   4, 30, 33, 35, 37, 38
Narmer   12, 13
Nasser, Gamal Abdel   30, 31, 32
National Democratic Party   33
National Unity Party   31
New Kingdom   14, 15
Nile River   10
Nile Valley   10
Nubians   15
Octavian   17
Old Kingdom   13, 15, 16
Ottoman Empire   23, 26, 28
Pepi II   16
Persians   16
Philo   18
Ptolemaic Dynasty   16, 17
Ptolemy   16
Ramses II   14
Rosetta Stone   24
Sadat, Anwar   32, 33
Saladin   21, 22
Sasanian Empire   19
Second Intermediate Period   14
Six-Day War   32
Suez Canal   27, 28, 29, 30, 31
Suleiman, Omar   33, 34
Tahrir Square   4, 7, 35
Thebes   13
Third Intermediate Period   15
Tutankhamun   15, 16
United Arab Republic   32
Wafd   29

About the Author

Russell Roberts has written and published nearly 50 books for adults and children, including *Larry Fitzgerald, The Building of the Panama Canal, The Cyclopes, Scott Joplin, The Battle of Waterloo,* and *Confucius.* He lives in Bordentown, New Jersey, with his family and a fat, fuzzy, and crafty calico cat named Rusti.